READING PUBS

JOHN DEARING

The
History
Press

First published 2009

The History Press
The Mill, Brimscombe Port
Stroud, Gloucestershire, GL5 2QG
www.thehistorypress.co.uk

Reprinted 2010

British Library Cataloguing in Publication Data.
A catalogue record for this book is available from the British Library.

ISBN 978 0 7524 5287 6

Typesetting and origination by The History Press
Printed in Great Britain

CONTENTS

ACKNOWLEDGEMENTS

The author would like to acknowledge the help given in various ways by Peter Durrant, Lisa Spurrier and the Berkshire Record Office, Anooshka Rawden and Reading Museum, David Cliffe and the Reading Local Studies Library, Ian Hamblin, Joan Hutchinson, Arthur Pounder, Roger Winslet, John Whitehead, Louise Cabread Jones, Nigel Sutcliffe, Raymond Quelch, Sidney Gold, the late Dr Judith Hunter, Mavis Wilkinson, William Hughes, Rhys Munday, Jane Marsden, Charlie Wheeler, Joe Wesolowski, Victor Wilson, Nick Hopton, Reginald Meade, Scott Nicol, Dorothy at the Red Cow, Bob Sawyer, Peter Jackson, Bill Westwood and any others I may not have mentioned. Thanks are also due to Mrs Mary Southerton, the History of Reading Society and Mrs Rita Noyes for access to two important collections of photographs, made by the late Peter Southerton and the late Doug Noyes, and to Bent Weber and Alan Copeland respectively for their assistance in this respect. Last but not least thanks to my publishers for their patient forbearance during an exceptionally long period of gestation for this work.

INTRODUCTION

Reading was a busy place in the Middle Ages and as such required the services of a number of hostelries for the accommodation and nourishment of visitors to the town and its abbey, not to mention their horses. The earliest of which we have records are the Bell (also known as the Guildhall), the Bear and the George, all mentioned in the fourteenth and fifteenth century Reading Guild accounts.

Although it bears the date 1506, the George in King Street is first mentioned in the will of Robert Bedewynde, Mayor from 1385-88, who left 'the reversion of the tenement called the "Georgesyn" in Reading to the Mayor of the vill of Reding for the time being.' The Guild accounts state that in 1512-13, payment of 5*d* was made at the George for 'bere and ale to my lord chamberleyns serjannts'. In the late 1540s it passed into the hands of William Gray, a friend of the Lord Protector Somerset under Edward VI and writer of the ballad, 'The Kynges Hunt is Upp'. In 1639 the 'George backside' was the scene of a riot, apparently caused by a fight over a dog.

In 1429-30 the Guild received 12*d* in rent from John Hende, together with a further 4*d* for 'rent of a new stable' at the Bell. In 1432-33 it was obliged to hire a carpenter for a day for the purpose of repairing the 'Gildhall inn' at a cost of 6*d*. In 1626, a runaway apprentice from London, Robert Woodd ran up a bill of 40*s* over four days at the Bell. He even had the cheek to tip the servants 4*s*! In 1636 it was one of several locations mentioned as 'scene of crime' when Johann Dambrell accused John Stevens of Dunsdew of getting her with child.

Another early arrival, now lost, was the Cardinal's Hat, where Reading's Protestant martyr, Julius Palmer, was arrested in 1556. The George must be regarded as the oldest of Reading's remaining public houses, although today it thrives more as a hotel and restaurant than as a pub in the normal sense.

The sixteenth century saw a great rise in the number of licensed premises nationwide and Reading was no exception. A census, taken in 1577, with a view to charging a 2*s* 6*d* tax on each public house to meet the cost of repairs to Dover Harbour, showed that Reading possessed seven inns, forty-four alehouses and three taverns, thus contributing £6.75 to the levy, roughly equivalent to £7,900 at present-day values. These fifty-four premises served a population of around 3,000.

Among the principal inns known to have existed in the seventeenth century were the Angel, (Black) Bear, Broad Face, Catherine Wheel, Crown, Olivant and Ship. An inn named the Sun also existed at this time, but there is evidence to suggest that this was located in the commercial area close to the Market Place, while the present Sun Inn in Castle Street seems to have originated as the Rising Sun around 1700. The Broad Face has the distinction of being mentioned by Samuel Pepys, who did not record the name of the inn he stayed at, where the service and entertainment displeased the great diarist. The Crown was patronised in the eighteenth century by the founder of Methodism, John Wesley, whose moral influence seems to have lingered, for in 1808 nearly 100 people met there to form a society 'for preaching the due observance of the Sabbath and the suppression of Vice and Immorality'.

Two inns in Reading bore the sign of the Bear, with the earliest recorded mention in 1483. The Black Bear was located in Bridge Street, close to the Kennet, while the Golden Bear may have stood at the north-western corner of Castle Street. It was well known for its cockpit, with matches fought every morning on Reading race days. In the mid-seventeenth century it was kept by a Mr Phipps, whose son, Sir Constantine, became Lord Chancellor of Ireland, and it was where the Mayor and Corporation entertained the Bishop of Salisbury in 1726. However, it had ceased trading and become a private house by 1802.

The Black Bear enjoyed a dubious reputation with at least one distinguished traveller. John Byng, Viscount Torrington, describes a night in July 1787 in the course of a ride into South Wales:

> … and were at the Black Bear, Reading, before our ladies arrived. Supper order'd, and quickly served, with a bowl (again) of sour and weak punch: we sat up till eleven o'clock, and were cheerful; but when I went to bed, I fancied the sheets damp and so to my sides there were only blankets.

The Bear also played its part in Reading's military history. In 1688 it was scene of the Battle of Reading. As Defoe wrote, this was 'a skirmish which saw the only blood drawn during the Glorious Bloodless Revolution' when 'the first party of Dutch found a company of foot soldiers drawn up in the church-yard over against the Bear Inn, and a troop of dragoons in the Bear Inn yard'. Over a century later, the poet Coleridge, escaping from creditors in Cambridge, enlisted in the 15th Light Dragoons under the unlikely name of Silas Tomkins Comberpatch and was billeted at the Bear Inn in December 1793. He is said to have been found out when he wrote a quotation from his Roman predecessor, the poet Boethius, on the stable wall to record his misery. A more infamous visitor was Governor Joseph Wall, who was held here in 1784 after his arrest for the murder by flogging of one of his troops in the African colony of Goree. He escaped through a window and subsequently evaded justice for eighteen years before suffering the due punishment of the law in 1802.

The Ship in Duke Street, sometimes referred to as the Upper Ship, receives an early mention in 1648, when the Oxford antiquary, Elias Ashmole, made merry there with two pheasants on St Valentine's Day. Forty years later, the birth of the Old Pretender was celebrated with 39s being paid for wine. In 1762 the *Reading Mercury* announced that a stagecoach, the Reading, Wokingham, Bracknell and Sunninghill Flying Machine was setting out on Mondays, Wednesdays and Fridays at 6 a.m. from the Upper Ship for Fleet Street, London. It was later a popular venue for political meetings, as when 300 farmers were addressed by William Cobbett in 1822 and when a meeting was held under the chairmanship of Colonel Blagrave in 1840 to rebut the anti-corn laws agitation, forming the Berkshire Association for the Protection of Agriculture.

Other houses of which we know very little other than the name and sometimes the location are the Broadgates; the Half Moon, where 'Danyell Pearce, vyntnier' pulled pints in 1612; the Hand; the Hat & Feather, mentioned in the probate inventory of Elizabeth Burd who died in 1748; the Hind Head in London Street, kept in 1600 by Richard Tench, a native of Shropshire who came to Reading to work in the cloth industry; and the Raven.

Old corporation records suggest that our forebears shared the same concerns as their descendants over such matters as full pints and licensing hours. In 1631, twelve publicans, including the 'Widowe Porter', were accused of having 'sould in their houses, severally, less than one full ale'. In 1652, William Greenwaie was prohibited to 'keepe alehouse or use common selling of ale or beere any longer' for the offence of 'suffering men to sitte drinking and tipling in his house on the lorde's daies.'

Pubs are inseparable from the products they sell, especially beer. Although many alehouses, as well as the abbey, would have brewed their own beer in the Middle Ages, the earliest recorded commercial brewing in Reading dates from the seventeenth century. The Castle Brewery was founded in 1698, became Blandy & Hawkins in the nineteenth century and after a brief period as part of the South Berkshire Brewery group, centred on Newbury, joined the Simonds empire in 1920.

William Blackall Simonds began his brewing enterprise in Broad Street in 1785 at the age of twenty-two, prospering sufficiently to move to a larger site in Bridge Street after a few years. Simonds was an astute businessman who involved himself in banking as well as brewing and was also a substantial landowner.

The development of coach travel in the eighteenth century gave a considerable boost to the licensed trade. In 1830 there were around sixteen coach services per day each way on the traditional route from London to Bath and Bristol. Coach travellers passing through Reading at this time were invited at the George to partake of a beverage known as 'Reading milk', which comprised a tumbler of milk laced with four tablespoons of rum and a lump of sugar, topped with grated nutmeg. Those who patronized the Crown were the first to sample Huntley & Palmer's biscuits, which were first manufactured at Mr Huntley's shop round the corner in London Street.

The Crown's primacy among Reading's inns in the early nineteenth century was illustrated in 1814 when 'public dinners' in celebration of the short-lived peace with France were held 'at the Crown Inn at 10s. 6d per head; at the Bear Inn at 5s 6d; at the Lower Ship at 2s 6d; and at many other places'. An evidently less prestigious dinner took place in April 1814 at 5s per head to celebrate the expiry of the property tax. In 1827 the successful Whig MP, Charles Fysshe Palmer, dined with 150 electors after a triumphal procession through the town, and he doubtless returned in 1832 when local Whigs met to celebrate the passing of the Reform Act.

Another inn that came to prominence during the coaching era was the Boar's Head in Friar Street, first mentioned in 1760. The first owner was Thomas Florey, who had been Mayor in 1749 and died in 1780. In 1785, it was acquired, along with its own brewery, by William Garrard, who also owned the Turks Head, Greyhound and Griffin and who gives his name to Garrard Street. Garrard declined to become Mayor on the grounds that it would cost him too much! In 1840 it was the scene of the inquest on Henry West, who was 'blown to his death in a whirlwind' while helping to build Reading Station. When sold in 1871, the inn was advertised as having six bedrooms, seven stables, four coach-houses, a malthouse and an abundant supply of excellent water. At that time it was popular with horse dealers using Benjamin Tompkin's Royal Horse and Carriage Repository next door.

The coming of the railways in the late 1830s brought about a rapid and terminal decline in the coaching traffic, although inns continued to serve the transport industry well into the twentieth century as depots for the numerous carrier services which linked Reading with the surrounding towns and villages. In 1834, the Bear was the scene of a meeting of local landowners to protest against the proposed Great Western Railway. This no doubt involved self-interest on the part of John James Tagg, who ran the inn, as the railways killed much of his trade. By 1842, he was advertising the fact that 'omnibuses, flys, phaetons and gigs await the arrival of every train'.

In the early nineteenth century, two factors provided a boost to the numbers of pubs – one local and one national. Reading itself began to expand considerably through its status as a major railway junction, growing from a population of 9,000 at the end of the eighteenth century to 50,000 a hundred years later. Developments such as New Town and the Watlington Street area to the east, and Whitley and Katesgrove to the south of the old town also brought with them the need for places of refreshment. In 1830, Parliament passed the Beer Act, which encouraged the establishment of beer houses with a licence for the retail of beer only. Simonds enjoyed strong connections with the gentry including the then Prime Minister, the Duke of Wellington, and it was evidently while hunting that he picked up the scent of this far-reaching new legislation. Accompanied by his groom, whose knowledge of local habits was invaluable, Simonds identified suitable sites for fifty new pubs while the bill was still going through Parliament, thus stealing a march on his rivals.

During the period 1880-1914, Reading's boundaries were extended to take in Caversham, along with much of Earley and Tilehurst, further increasing the number of pubs.

However, the twentieth century proved to be a time of decline, particularly as the town centre and the slum area of Coley became depopulated in the post-war period. Out of sixty-four public houses located in an area broadly constituting the town centre that flourished between 1931 and 1956, nearly half (thirty-one) have disappeared, and many obliterated to create the Inner Distribution Road (IDR). A further four are currently closed and twelve used for other purposes, leaving seventeen that are trading. Some are under different names and not all are conventional public houses. This process was slower to get underway in the residential areas of the town, but the 1990s and early 2000s have also seen reductions in numbers in these areas. This has been fuelled partly by 'asset-stripping' on the part of brewers and 'pubcos', partly by pressures to create more housing and partly by difficulties faced by landlords of local pubs in remaining competitive against new town centre mega-pubs, especially in the face of unsympathetic legislation and fiscal policies emanating from central government.

The mega-pubs began to appear in the early 1990s and there are now around thirty such houses in the town centre and the Oracle development on the Simonds Brewery site. Although most are open to the general public, few other than the three outlets of the J.D. Wetherspoon organisation can in any sense be considered conventional pubs. Typically they appeal to a narrow cross-section of the community, those under twenty-five, and tend not to serve traditional ales.

Nevertheless, the author likes to think that the conviction that 'small is beautiful' is one that reigns somewhere in the heart of even the most hedonistic young reveller and that small community locals have by no means had their day. He himself does his best to support them.

1

INNS OF THE COACHING ERA AND EARLIER

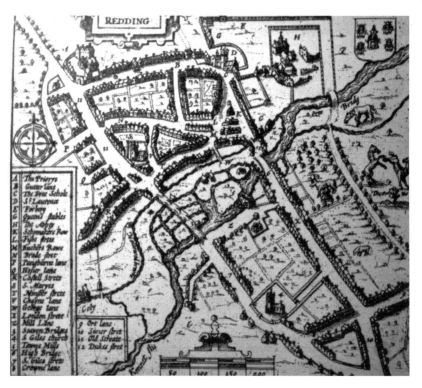

John Speed's map of Reading is dated 1610 and shows a town that had then changed little from the Middle Ages, with a population of around 5,000. Many of the oldest inns whose names are recorded disappeared without trace during the next two centuries as the town expanded and road widening took place to accommodate traffic.

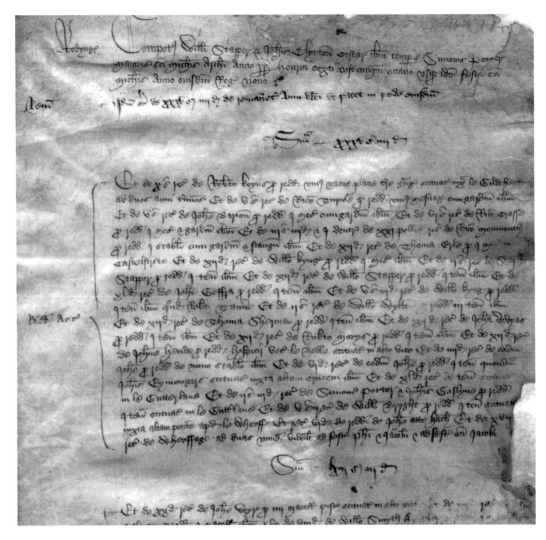

The Bell, also known as the Guildhall Inn, vies with the George for the honour of being Reading's oldest recorded hostelry. It was situated in the High Street and owned by the Guild, the predecessor body to the Town Council. Reference to the Bell is made in the Guild accounts for 1429-30.

Opposite: The Angel at 117 Broad Street developed from a sixteenth-century brewhouse to become, by 1785, a leading coaching inn. This was the date when the new 'flying' coach service from the Angel Inn to the Bolt & Tun, Fleet Street was announced in the *Reading Mercury*. Later it was the starting point for Royal Forester coaches to London, the Original Dart to Oxford via Abingdon and Pinnock's service to Southampton.

cellars.

Alfo, adjoining fo immediately connected, as to be made either a part of the Great Houfe, or to be a diftinct Tenement; confifting on the firft floor, of four convenient bed-chambers, with garrets; on the ground floor, an hall, two parlours, kitchen, larder, beer cellar, laundry, and wafh houfe; coach-houfe, and ftables, with a garden walled in. The prefent tenant, Mr. Herfchell, to the laft mentioned premifes will quit on Michaelmas day next.

For further particulars, enquire of William Reddington, Windfor; where tickets may be had to fhew the premifes.

The PROPRIETORS of the

Reading Poft-Coaches and Machine,

From the ANGEL INN,

BEG leave to acquaint the public, that on Monday the 11th inftant they began flying, from whence

A   P O S T - C O A C H

will fet out every morning at feven o'clock, and return from the Bolt and Tun, Fleet-ftreet, every afternoon at half paft one.

And for the further accommodation,

A   P O S T - C O A C H

will fet out from the Angel Inn every afternoon at half paft one o'clock.

A   P O S T - C O A C H

will fet out every morning from the Bolt and Tun, Fleet-ftreet, at fix o'clock, and be at Reading to dinner.

F L Y I N G   M A C H I N E

will fet out every morning at five o'clock, and return from the Bolt and Tun at twelve o'clock precifely.

* Thefe Poft-Coaches and Machine will always call at the Old White Horfe Cellar, Piccadilly; where paffengers are taken up, and parcels carefully booked and delivered.

SMITH and WEALE, Proprietors.

BASINGSTOKE RACES, 1785.

ON Thurfday the 9th of June, will be run for on Bafingftoke Down, 50l. for any four-year old horfe, &c. that never won 50l. (matches and fweepftakes excepted) colt 8ft. 3lb. fillies 8ft. The beft of three heats, two miles and a diftance to each heat.—To ftart at the diftance chair.

Same day, a fweepftakes of 25 guineas each, by four-year olds, 8ft. 4lb. five-year olds, 9ft. fix-year olds 9ft. 6lb. and aged 9ft. 9lb.—Two miles. Thofe that have not won 50l. in plate or match before the 1ft. of January, 1785, to be allowed 3lb. mares to carry 3lb. lefs than horfes.—The winner to be fold for 200gs. if demanded within a quarter of an hour after the race, the owner of the fecond horfe being firft intitled, &c.

Lord Stawell's ch. g. by Eclipfe, aged.

Mr. Thiftlethwayte's gr. c. Squib, by Piftol, 4 years old.

From 1820 until 1863 the Angel was run by William Parsons. It was then acquired by W.H. Ferguson & Sons, who commissioned the architect, William Brown, to design additions and alterations in 1863 and 1870. The Angel Brewery, also known as Fergusons, operated for some fifty years till 1914, when Morlands of Abingdon took control and brewing of 'Anglo-Saxon Beer and Nourishing Stout' ceased. The Angel itself was demolished in 1964 and the site is now occupied by British Home Stores and Clinton Cards.

In the first half of the nineteenth century the Bear was run by the Tagg family, beginning with James Tagg (died 1817), who took over the old Bear in 1801 and was formerly cook to the 2nd Viscount Palmerston, father of the future Prime Minister. By 1827, John James Tagg was the licensee and also operated his own brewery on the site from 1828 to 1856, when succeeded by another James Tagg. The family's tombs can be seen in St Giles' Churchyard.

Above: The new Bear was completed in 1811. In 1826 it was host to a party including the Lord Mayor of London who arrived from Oxford in the State Barge. Four years later a grand dinner was held to mark the retirement of Dr Richard Valpy as Master of Reading School.

Right: The Bear declined in importance with the passing of the stage-coach era and was taken over by Simonds Brewery in 1897 and partly demolished in 1910. With Bert Rex as the last landlord, it finally closed its doors in 1938 to become brewery offices. The licence and name passed to a new pub in Tilehurst. It finally disappeared from the landscape in 1983, but its name has been preserved in a new housing development on the Kennet named 'Bear Wharf'.

The Black Horse on the corner of London Street and Queens Road is first mentioned in 1711. In 1809, during the May Fair, the inn 'was robbed of notes to the value of upwards of £15' when 'the town was infested by mendicants and thieves'. Later it was described as 'an old established Inn with large stable accommodation, situated in a good position in Reading' but it ended up as the lost property office for Reading Corporation Transport.

William Garrard's sons sold his brewery and pubs including the Boar's Head to Hewett's Brewery – as depicted they eventually became part of Courages. Popularly known as the 'Whore's Bed', it survived a number of threats to its existence before being demolished in 2004 for a hotel development of stultifying mediocrity.

The Broad Face in the High Street is said to have been one of only two inns to bear the Broad Face sign; the example in Abingdon being the sole survivor. On his only recorded visit to Reading in the summer of 1668, Samuel Pepys spotted '... one odd sign of the Broad Face. Then to my inn, and so to bed'. It was demolished in 1926 and Lloyd's Bank now occupies the site.

Above: A Black Bull is mentioned in the 1740s and is possibly to be identified with the inn in Church Street near St Giles' where, in April 1810, 'The Worthy Knights of the Order of Malt & Hops held at Sir James Faulkner's the Bull' were bidden to attend their the Quarterly Dinner. Better known to later generations of pub-goers was the Bull Hotel at 23 Broad Street, at the corner of Cross Street, kept in 1852 by Joseph Pecover.

Left: In the 1950s Raymond Quelch had his first pint of Bass in the Bull when it was kept by Bill, an 'ex-naval officer' who 'was behind the bar, with brilliant white shirt, black tie, blazer and grey trousers with razor sharp creases in keeping with naval traditions.' The pub closed in 1975 because according to Bass 'it stood on a prime high street site' – but the bull itself can still be seen in the upper reaches of the building.

In 1831, the Castle Inn in Castle Street was claimed to be 'the principal inn where the Bath and Bristol coaches stop at Reading'. Long-distance services using the inn at this time included the Chronometer – London to Bath, Bristol, Exeter and Plymouth; the Royal Magnet and the Emerald, both London to Bath. The Listed building at 17 Castle Street, shown here and currently solicitors' offices, has been claimed as the Castle Inn but seems more likely to have been the home of the brewer at the Castle Brewery.

The later building of this name is shown here. In 1888 the innkeeper, Charles Kearl, summonsed Henry Allan for being 'drunk and disorderly and refusing to quit'. Allan was fined 10s with 10s costs, with the alternative of fourteen days' hard labour.

Above and opposite above: The Crown at the corner of London Street and Crown Street is first mentioned in 1518. In 1630, a man of Kent staying at the inn was accused of spending three or four days in the town 'from alehouse to alehouse without any business' but claimed in defence that 'the cause of his staye was to cure his horse.' More respectable later visitors included John Wesley, a frequent caller on his preaching journeys (pictured here), William Pitt, the Princess Amelia and in 1816, the Duke and Duchess of Orleans.

The Elephant in Market Place originally took the older form of 'Olivant'. In January 1809 'John Wicks, a bargeman and an old offender, was convicted of stealing a great coat from the "Elephant"... and was sentenced to be transported for 7 years'. It was used by carriers in the nineteenth century and was also the Reading terminus of an early omnibus service. Here it is seen with the Royal Standard next door, dwarfed by later buildings including Sutton's Seeds.

Above and below: The Elephant was rebuilt in the Victorian age in an 'exuberant chequered brick'. Early in the 1900s it was patronised by a travelling dentist who pulled teeth out painlessly for 1s. The last landlord was Luciano 'Lucky' Noventa, before the pub closed in 1968 to be replaced by offices.

Right and below: Something of the ambience of a coaching inn still lingers around the George. It was used by the Telegraph to London via Maidenhead daily; the Rocket to Southampton three times weekly; and the Star to Bath and Bristol. Later Dickens was a visitor, using the George as a stopping-off point on journeys to the south-west during his reading tours.

Above: The Horn stands at the corner of Castle Street and St Mary's Butts and is believed to date from the seventeenth century, although its earliest mention as a hostelry is in 1823 when John Pecover was landlord. In 1917 and 1918 the Horn raised 8s ½d and £1 10s 6d respectively for the Royal Berkshire Hospital in response to its Comforts for Wounded Soldiers appeal.

Left: The Horn was one of six Reading pubs to appear in CAMRA's first *Good Beer Guide* in 1974, when it was characterised as a 'popular friendly pub within sight of the brewery.' Dolly Mitchell, Reading's oldest resident at the time of her death in 2000, 'used to enjoy a couple of glasses of lunchtime Guinness in the Horn' with a bottle of draught-mild to take home in an empty whisky bottle'. Her nephew, Ian, is seen here with mostly departed former chums.

The Horse & Jockey, 120 Castle Street, is first mentioned in 1699 but was rebuilt in 1823. It was a house of call for wagons and coaches, being listed in 1825 as a stopping place for Baker & Gilder's London to Newbury coaches, and in 1837 as the loading point for Basing's wagon from Frome to London. The wagon shown here may be bound for the Horse & Jockey.

For about seven years up to 1999, Peter and Val Taylor were popular landlord and lady, winning the Reading Pub of the Year award from CAMRA twice.

Left: Greene King purchased the Horse & Jockey but sold it on in 2002 to Outside Inns, who renamed it as 120 Castle Street. Happily, it has more recently resumed its traditional name.

Below: The Mitre was originally near St Laurence's Church and Blandy's solicitors, but later moved to West Street. In the latter part of the nineteenth century it had its own brewery, with William Newell as resident brewer. By 1903 it had passed into the hands of the Wallingford Brewery, which was acquired by Ushers in 1928. It is now the Thai Corner restaurant.

The most imposing of Reading's former inns, the King's Arms, Castle Hill, was only an inn for some seventy years from the mid-eighteenth century. It features in Mary Russell Mitford's *Belford Regis* as the scene of a weekly whist drive.

In 1796, the King's Arms was requisitioned by the government as a hostel for Norman clergy fleeing from the French revolution. More than 340 priests were billeted there, forty of whom died during their years of exile. The assembly room was used as a chapel. Today it is known as Jersey House.

The Peacock in Broad Street was perhaps the last inn built to serve the coaching trade, for it was described as 'nearly new' in 1831, when it had eleven bedrooms, stabling for thirty-two horses and a skittle ground. Its landlord in the late nineteenth century, James Nelson Wernham, was a pioneer of public transport in Reading, setting up several horse-bus routes linking with other hostelries such as the Prince of Wales, Caversham and the Queens Head, Christchurch Green. He used the slogan 'Forward without fear'. The Peacock was demolished in 1922 to make way for a Woolworth's store.

The Royal Oak was in Fisher Row, later part of Broad Street, on a site now occupied by Marks & Spencer. In 1808, it was one of three inns where 'Mr Lewis and the inhabitants ... entertained the Danish prisoners of war'. A friendly society named The United Brethren met there in the 1820s. Latterly, as shown here, it had the Victoria Café as its next-door neighbour.

The Ship survives as a hotel to this day, having been largely rebuilt in 1912, and currently trades as the Royal County Hotel.

Corporation records refer to an inn called the Starr in 1631, a veritable den of iniquity. The Star in Duke Street has been dated to the mid-eighteenth century. In 1840, PC Webb was dismissed from the force for drunkenness and 'consorting with common prostitutes' in the Star Public House. Rebuilt in 1868 for Langtons of Maidenhead, it was latterly owned by Allied Breweries. Elizabeth Hurley is said to have been a customer around 1980. The Star closed in 1984, and the Grosvenor Casino which has its own bar was later built on the site. Its name survives in Star Lane.

Originally known as the Rising Sun, the Sun was probably developed into an inn from existing properties around 1700 by John Westmoreland, a Reading clothier. Around 1807 it was the scene of a recruitment drive by Lord Paget's Hussars, whose recruitment poster promised that 'The Honors and Comforts attached to the life of a Hussar are innumerable; he has everything that he can possibly wish for found him, without any trouble to himself.' A notable feature of the Sun's architecture was its underground stables, which were entered from an ancient doorway which may have survived from a former friary.

The underground hall provided stabling for fifty horses, but in the motor age these were used as storage for the cast of circuses and other entertainments. The rampaging of the elephants from Bertram Mills Circus is believed to have led to the structure collapsing in 1947, fortunately on the day after the Mayor and Mayoress had paid a visit.

From 1876 till his death in 1916 the redoubtable Charles Roberts kept the Sun. He was also a farmer and a keen man of the turf with a race-horse, said to have competed in the Cesarewitch and the Derby. He died as a result of a fall while hunting. During his tenure the pub came under the South Berks Brewery.

Although it did not feature greatly in the coaching trade, the Sun was a major centre for the carriers who served the outlying villages around Reading, a traffic that continued until just after the Second World War. By then it was part of Simonds, later Courage.

The elephants are seen marching through Broad Street in 1897.

The oldest Swan, possibly the Black Swan, seems to have been in Broad Street. In 1635, Richard Hawkes was 'forbidden' for disorder at this hostelry. The White Swan was possibly the one located at 23/24 St Mary's Butts and seems to have been called plain Swan after the Black Swan closed in the mid-nineteenth century.

The Swan was rebuilt in 1889 to designs of G.W. Webb for Hawkins' Brewery. After being used for other commercial purposes for many years, including Rediffusion and a shop selling rattan furniture, it has resumed its career as Pavlov's Dog in the youth-oriented It's a Scream chain, originally part of the Bass Group.

The Turk's Head in London Road originally comprised two cottages which are mentioned in the Royal Charter granted to Reading in 1559. In the early nineteenth century, its address was 18 Albion Street. In 1814, 'a post-chaise, belonging to Mr Frankland, standing at the Turk's Head, the horses took fright and ran away.' In 1816 a new coach service started by 'a party of tradesmen' of the town was launched from the Turk's Head with a crowd of 1,000 coming to watch. The inn is depicted in a famous print of 1823 by William Henry Timms.

Eddie and Morie Colhane were licensees of the Turk's Head from the late 1960s until John Bibby took over in 1983. During his tenure the pub received the first of two extensions but retained much of its character until 1996 when it was renamed the Fez & Firkin, following Allied Breweries' acquisition of the Firkin chain. With the demise of the Firkin concept the pub resumed half of its original name in 2002, becoming the Turks. The premises once sported a mummified cat which was stolen by high-spirited medical students. The flying snowman appears to uphold that tradition.

Fez & Firkin was one of several names half-jokingly submitted by the writer.

The White Hart at 1 Oxford Road is mentioned in 1810 when Richard Frewin returned to his former pub from the Boar's Head. The White Hart boasted stables for forty carrier horses and six mail horses and a milestone in the tap room which indicated that it was fifteen miles to Wallingford. A Blandy & Hawkins pub, it was rebuilt in 1902 to a design by G.W. Webb but this was in turn replaced during road widening in 1932-33. In the late 1930s the 'new pub' embodied Reading's 'first American style snack bar' which was for a time the 'in' place for the more affluent younger set. However, by the early 1950s it was where Irish navvies used to congregate looking for work from subcontractors. In 1968 it gave way to the Butts Centre.

2

LATER TOWN CENTRE PUBS

The Alfred's Head in Chatham Street is seen here on its last legs as a pub. A one-time Wethered's pub, it has since become an ethnic restaurant.

The Allied Arms at 57 St Mary's Butts is a Grade II Listed building which has been dated to the sixteenth century. Rear outbuildings are said to incorporate remains of a former nunnery, including a well. However, it only appears to have become a pub in 1828. As shown in the watercolour by Louise Rayner, it incorporated a brewery between 1878 and 1890, when Thomas Jerome was brewer, specializing in Home Brewed Stout.

At one time the bar window depicted the flags of England, France and Turkey, being the allies in question in the Crimean War – when Turkey ceased to be an ally it was painted out! The present pub sign seems to point to an earlier conflict.

In the 1960s the Allied was frequented by Irishmen working on the construction of the M4 and one landlord reportedly caused a riot by calling time two minutes early! In the 1980s, Albert Smith was a popular landlord succeeded for a time by his widow.

After a number of shorter tenancies, the pub was taken over by Steve and Moya Rolls in 2001 and has since become a popular 'real ale' outlet in the town.

The Anchor stood at the corner of London Street and Albion Street, now London Road. Thomas Harbor, whose son enlisted in the 7th Hussars during the Peninsular War, was landlord for nearly thirty years. Later, Daniel Toovey presided for twenty years. The pub's demolition was recommended in the interests of road safety, but Frank Eyles next door survived till the 1980s as Reading's last pawnbroker.

The Barley Mow, 55 London Street, was a pub before the nineteenth century and was an unofficial HQ of the Tory party during the 1812 Election when 'a butt of strong beer was drawn on a truck and left opposite' to elicit favour from voters. 'A clumsy fellow in tapping it lost a lot, which escaped into the gutter and thence into the throats of "some of the roughs"'. It was the venue for meetings of the Hand in Hand, a friendly society in the 1820s.

Despite frequent changes of landlord with twenty-five during the nineteenth century, of which Thomas Oldfield (1806-23) stayed the longest, the Barley Mow did not close till the early 1980s. The buildings were subsequently occupied by a firm of solicitors and Amethyst wines and later, as shown here, estate agents.

The Beehive Commercial Hotel was located at 169 Friar Street and was where Charles Martin also operated a brewery in the mid-nineteenth century. An advertisement has him 'returning thanks to his Friends and the Public for their liberal support since he commenced Brewing'. Here it is nervously sandwiched between a dairy and a butcher's.

The Britannia Tap at 50-52 Caversham Road and the Britannia Hotel opposite were both demolished in the 1980s for office development. The Tap was originally the tap bar of the Britannia Brewery, also in Caversham Road, which flourished from 1850 to 1896 with Walter Julian Pain as the brewer for the last twenty years. It was then bought out by Ind Coope. Just before the Second World War, Fred Doddington, former Traffic Superintendent for Thackray's, the pioneering coach company, became landlord.

Opposite above and below: The Bugle, 144 Friar Street, is the last remaining traditional pub in Friar Street. Early landlords included David Daniel as proprietor, James Simmonds and Elizabeth Davis. A Simonds pub for many years, it still sells Courage branded beers. The pub sign shows a bugler of the 66th (Berkshire) Regiment at the famous battle of Maiwand.

Ye Butcher's Arms stood at the Butts end of Hosier Street and was ultimately redeveloped as part of Butts Centre. This was a Wethered house, for which J.H. Deacon of Marlow designed stabling and stores in 1898.

The Butler, 43 Chatham Street, began life as the Baker's Arms but by 1839 it had come into the hands of the Butler family and thereafter became known as Butler's Wine Vaults, or just plain Butler's.

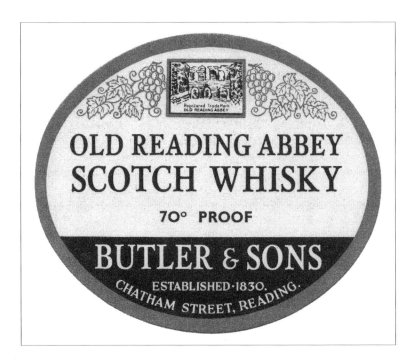

Above and below: Butler's was famous (or some would say infamous) for its wines and other concoctions produced in its bottling plant (see labels). The author has been informed that Butler's Mountain Wine (otherwise known as 'Rocket Fuel') was considered an acceptable alternative to a Watney's Party Seven to take to a party you were gate-crashing.

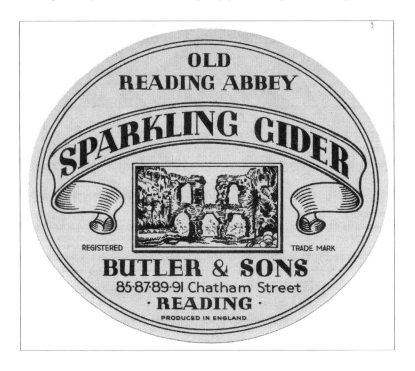

Above and left: The premises were acquired by Fuller's and opened as the Butler in 1977, with Bernard Butler pulling the first pint and beer sold at 1952 prices in this Jubilee Year. All connection with the Butler family seems lost in the present inn sign.

The Cheddar Cheese at 124 Broad Street was called the Boar's Head in the nineteenth century and possibly acquired its new name when Simonds bought the property to distinguish it from the Boar's Head in Friar Street. In the 1920s George W. Smith promoted his pub with the following doggerel:

Here's a place where you can sit at ease,
While 'Mine Host' does his utmost to please …
SIMONDS' Bitter, Stout and their famous S.B.'S:
To really enjoy all these,
COME TO THE CHEDDAR CHEESE.

Latterly it was known for its upstairs bar 'with lots of mirrors, chrome and maple wood veneers'.

The Cock Inn, Fisher Row, now Broad Street, reputedly dates from around 1565 but was renamed the London Tavern around 1845 and the Hobgoblin in 1994. In 1901 it was refaced after the original frontage collapsed. In the 1950s, when Bill and Gwen Fulton ran the pub, it was haunted by a strange man called the Lemonade Man because he drank eight pints of lemonade each session.

In the 1970s the London Tavern was well-known for its businessmen's lunches and in the 1980s it was run by Steve Ellyatt, who later bought the Tanners Arms. After some years of decline it reopened as a Wychwood Brewery pub in 1993 and since then has been a favourite with real ale drinkers as the Hobgoblin, as the fine display of pump-clips testifies.

Frank Wicks was one of the characters using the Hobgoblin who is still remembered with affection.

The first landlord for Wychwood, Duncan Ward, wanted the pub to be called the Campaign Arms but the brewery had other ideas. The Hobgoblin can justly claim to have served more different beers than any other pub in the town.

Although the Coopers at 29-31 Market Place is a Grade II Listed building, it only became a pub in the 1960s, having previously been Lewis (later Arthur) Cooper's wine shop. It was for a while part of the Rat & Parrot chain, but subsequently returned to its previous name. There are currently redevelopment plans that will affect the pub, but they are expected to retain some licensed premises. One wit in past days is said to have claimed that there was a right of way to drive livestock to market through the corridor that then separated two bars and made his case by walking along it with a piglet tied to a lead.

On the corner of Gun Street and Bridge Street, the Cross Keys was rebuilt in the later nineteenth century, partly to the designs of Brown and Albury, when G.F. Shadbolt was the landlord. Subsequently acquired by Morlands, it was one of six Reading pubs in CAMRA's first *Good Beer Guide* of 1974, described as a 'street corner pub with strong Irish influence'. On one 'Irish' occasion a passer-by is said to have been nearly hit by a chair which was projected through a window – he grabbed it and threw it back through another window!

Just as town centre pubs were coming back into fashion, the Cross Keys was sold off by the brewery in 1989 and it has since served younger drinkers under various names, latterly Sahara's. However, its fine exterior playing on the cross keys theme can still be admired.

The Fox, 24 West Street, was a Simonds house, a new building being designed for them by Brown and Albury in 1881. This was short-lived as it lost its licence and was closed in 1914, being replaced by the Maypole Dairy until 1939 and later by a succession of shoe shops. The old pub was mentioned in an assault case in 1852.

Opposite above: The pub at 82 London Street began life as the Goat, but over seventy-five years changed to the Lamb, Duke of Wellington, Post Boy, Grapes and finally the Acorn, with twenty changes of landlord. John Josey's tenure was the only one to reach double figures. During the Peninsular War it was the headquarters of the 'Buffs' recruiting party, but in 1814 it was 'indicted as an house of ill-fame'. After 1877 it was demolished and replaced by premises used for light engineering and cycle manufacture, part of which is now a Nepalese restaurant.

Opposite below: The Duke's Head, 41/ 42 Broad Street, was demolished in 1933 with a Joe Lyons restaurant occupying part of the site until 1969. Since then, clothing and shoe shops have prevailed. Frederick Dakin, followed by Mrs Dakin, presumably his widow, were long-serving licensees at the turn of the nineteenth century.

...ing. King Edward VII Statue.

Kennet House, 2 London Street, is depicted in the centre of this Timms print to the south of the High Bridge. Originally used by a coach-building and harness-making outfit, it became a pub in 1836 with its own brewhouse up to around 1850.

Opposite above: The Great Western Hotel, Station Road, founded in 1842, is said to have been designed by Brunel himself, although lesser mortals have been suggested as more likely. It was originally known as the Railway Hotel and Tap. In 1860, Grand Duke Michael of Russia, brother to the Tsar, breakfasted at the hotel with a large entourage on the way to Torquay, to visit his sick wife. The Russian connection continued when, in 1945, Churchill and Eden stopped for tea on their way back from the Yalta Conference.

Opposite below: In 1954, the Great Western was acquired by Trust Houses Forte, who closed it in 1972 to be replaced by the new Post House near the M4. Happily, listing prevented the demolition of this fine building. Thirty years on, after use as offices, it has been reopened as a hotel by the Malmaison group.

Later, Henry Coggs was the landlord for many years, followed by Mrs Coggs and towards the end of the century, Albert and Esther Wheeler. The building now houses the London Street Brasserie.

The Kennet Arms, Castle Street, was known as 'The Kennet Brewery' in 1871 when John Edwards was the innkeeper. In 1888, Charles Norman was fined £5 for permitting drunkenness on his licensed premises, with twenty-one days' imprisonment 'in default of distress'. It closed in 1969 to make way for the Inner Distribution Road (IDR).

To the north of the High Bridge at 22 Duke Street, the Lower Ship was also known as Horse and Barge, although this print by Timms of 1823 shows its name then as Lower Ship. In 1789 the artist's father, William Timms, had kept the pub, announcing that he had 'lately entered the wine and spirit trade which he sells wholesale and retail'.

In 1889 it was rebuilt by Nicholson & Son, the Maidenhead brewers, to designs by Frederick W. Albury (1845-1912). However, it closed in the early 1980s and has been boarded up ever since.

Above: The Malthouse in Greyfriars Road was a noted gay pub as the Tudor Arms and has more recently resumed its connections with the gay community. It owes its current appearance to alterations designed by Gerald Berkeley Wills in 1937 intended to improve what had been 'a fair example of the poorer type of public-house of about fifty years ago.'

Left: The Nags Head, Russell Street was formerly a Morlands pub with a very strong Irish influence. After disposal by Greene King, it reopened as a free house in 2007 with a strong commitment to cask ales and grew in popularity.

The Oasis in Baker Street, formerly the Eagle, is one of the most recent Reading pubs to close, but is shown here in a mood of patriotic fervour.

The Oatsheaf at 46 Broad Street, now the premises of a building society, was a 1932 rebuilding to the order of Simonds, but the site is believed to have been the house of Archbishop William Laud, born in Reading in 1573. From 1850 to 1906 it was also the location of Dowsett's Brewery. The design has the hint of a Dutch-style gable and unusual window layout, possibly based on Laud's house. The pub used to be next to the Vaudeville Cinema.

Left: The Simonds hop leaf turns up everywhere!

Below: Like the nearby Ancient Foresters, Ye Old Friars at 63 Friar Street was a Blatch's house. In 1937, Mr and Mrs T.A. May were behind the bar serving customers when 'a thief apparently walked through from the bar into the living room' and then 'walked out with a quantity of jewellery.'

Above and below: The Post Office Tavern at 96 Broad Street, on the corner of Chain Street, took its name from Reading's first GPO on the opposite corner. Thomas Rosier was the last landlord in 1900 when, possibly as a result of illicit gambling, it was closed and transformed into Poynder's Post Office Bookshop and Library. From 1919 it was an upmarket men's outfitters for over seventy years.

Above: Occasionally the original name of the Post Office Tavern turns up during makeovers.

Opposite above and below: The Prince of Wales occupied the corner of Chatham Street and Thorn Street. At one time a Morlands beerhouse, it was run by the Brunsden family from 1933 until its closure in 1968, when it was demolished to make way for the IDR. Oak panelling from the pub was incorporated into an extension to the Gardeners Arms, Emmer Green. Performers at the Palace Theatre are said to have stayed at the Prince. The photographs show it as a thriving pub, and in the centre of a building site shortly before demolition.

The Queens Arms, Great Knollys Street, is the only survivor of three pubs in Reading to bear this name; the others were in Friar Street and Hosier Street. Like the nearby Lion, it enjoyed an all-day licence on cattle market days before all-day opening was legalised.

Opposite below: The Railway Tavern was one of the rare survivors of the piecemeal redevelopment of Greyfriars Road in the 1980s, but was turned into an Irish theme pub, Scruffy Murphys, and was later renamed the Gateway. In 1978, new licensees Gordon and Valerie Gowers introduced a new pub sign, replacing Stephenson's Rocket with a High Speed 125 diesel-electric loco.

The pub in Minster Street originally called the Queens Head had become known as the Pelican by 1840. However in 1856, it was taken over by Charles Francis Oliver and became known thereafter as Oliver's. George Tame took over as manager in 1906 and under him the name 'Reindeer' was first adopted in 1920. The last landlord before the pub closed in 1961, to make room for extensions to Heelas' store, was Alfred Frank Knell, who was renowned for his bread, cheese and pickles. When he left he was presented with a wine cabinet by customers.

The Rising Sun, Forbury Road, was built on the site of the Chapel of the Resurrection, Reading's first Roman Catholic place of worship since the Reformation. It was rebuilt in 1877 to designs by Brown and Albury for the Greys Brewery. For long a Brakspears pub, it later served as a Tut 'n' Shive theme pub but has recently been refurbished by Brakspears.

Opposite: The former Sailor's Home in West Street was empty for many years before reopening as a fast-food outlet. In 1888, Henry Champion was charged with stealing a waistcoat valued at 10s from landlord James Gale. In 1964, it was redesigned as the Captain's Cabin to resemble such quarters in Nelson's day. After being vandalised by football louts, its name was changed first to the Admiral and then in rapid succession, the Dagmar, Zigis and the Office.

The Shades was next to the Oracle workhouse at 15 Gun Street, as depicted in this 1840 painting. By the time the latter was demolished in 1850, it was already a pub. Originally called the Old Dolphin, it incorporated a lock-up used by the night-watchman to detain any prisoners he arrested. Arthur Oliver, the landlord in the 1830s-40s, changed its name to the Shades. In 1879, under the heading 'Keeping Open Beyond Hours', it was reported that 'Edward Bennett, landlord ... was charged with opening his house for the sale of beer at 11.45 pm on the 31st of March.' [Copyright Reading Museum Service (Reading Borough Council). All rights reserved.]

Having closed as a pub in 1958, the Shades became the English Grill in 1971. Later renamings include the Dutch House, Cartoons, Oscars and the Raj.

Above: The Traveller's Friend, 136-37 Friar Street was originally a Ferguson's house, later Morlands. At one time the pub had a ladies' bar but it was knocked into the lounge as few ladies used it. In 1940, William Frederick Lucas of this pub was fined 10*s* for allowing a light to show during the black-out.

Left: From 1959 until his death in 1987 it was run by Bob Roper, a South African who had served over twenty years in the British army. Sadly it did not long survive Mr Roper, for along with the Cross Keys, it was sold by Morlands in 1989 for commercial use and is now an employment bureau.

The Truro Brewery Tap at 46 Castle Street was a beerhouse associated with the brewery that was for many years owned by the Justins-Brinn family. Fergusons Ltd bought the brewery from William James Justins-Brinn in 1900, along with its thirty public houses. One of its later landlords was Alf Messer, captain of the Reading Royals during their promotion year of 1925/26.

The Truro pub continued till 1973, but this view dating from 1972 shows the bulldozer getting closer. The site is now occupied by the Police Station.

The former Marquess of Lorne at 125 Friar Street derived its name from the courtesy title of the Duke of Argyll prior to his succession to the dukedom. After his death in 1914, it was redesigned by George Reginald Morris, architect and surveyor to H. & G. Simonds, in the Tudor style, and as a result it became known as the Tudor Tavern. A well-known jazz pub in the 1980s, it rapidly declined thereafter and was recently converted for other retail use.

The Vine Hotel, situated on the corner of West Street and Broad Street, was replaced in the early 1930s by Burton's tailors and the site is now a newspaper and convenience shop. In 1884, the ubiquitous Brown and Albury designed a billiard room for the Vine. There was also at one time a pub of the same name in Grape Passage off Hosier Street. Here, the crowds are out for the opening of the electric tram service in 1903.

Opposite above: The Victory, Bedford Road belonged to the Greys Brewery and was acquired by Brakspears with the brewery in 1896. It was closed in 1963, with the licence transferred to a new Brakspears pub of the same name in Tilehurst. This in turn has closed, but the original Victory still stands, the premises of Hills Rubber Co.

Opposite below: The Wallingford Arms in Caroline Street was a former Morlands pub. In the 1990s the landlord had a loveable rottweiler called Guinness, who would often be found sprawled across the floor. Following its closure in 2005 it featured in the abduction of a Reading teenager who was later savagely murdered.

The Wellington Arms at the corner of Howard Street and Soho Street was one of the several pubs kept by the enterprising James N. Wernham, proprietor in 1871. It was later run for many years by George James Greenaway.

Wellman's Wine Vaults. Despite the rather posh name, this small Minster Street pub opposite the George was famous in its latter days for a gas fire that was little short of lethal and for the depths of nicotine coating its walls – if you touched them an impression of your hand would appear.

3

THE EXPANSION OF
READING

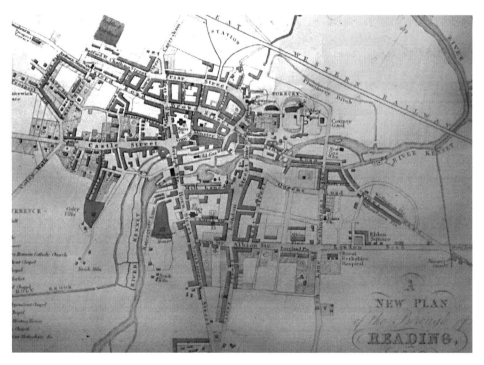

This 1840 map shows Reading beginning to grow. Old Coley to the west and Newtown and St Johns to the east were the first areas outside the immediate town centre to expand – and to spawn pubs. Newtown was largely rebuilt in the 1970s and now has only one pub, while much of Old Coley ended up under the IDR at the turn of the 1960s.

One of the most notorious houses in Old Coley was the Blue Lion, Wolseley Street, formerly Union Terrace, Coley Street. On one occasion a bobby who tried to break up a fight outside the pub was thrown into the Holybrook. In 1903 this Simonds pub was rebuilt to designs by Ravenscroft, Son & Morris.

The imposing new pub closed on 1 January 1969 to make way for the IDR and the luckless last landlord, Mr P.A. Hodder, moved to the Little Crown, which also closed later in the year. It is shown here with the nearby Rose & Crown.

Other Coley pubs, many of which disappeared long before the bulldozers came on the scene, included the Brickmakers Arms in Brickfield Terrace, the Bricklayer's Arms, the Crown and John Bull in Coley Place, the Coachmakers Arms, Three Goats and Turners Arms, all in Coley Street, the Borough Arms, Willow Street (shown here) and the Wooden Walls of Old England.

St Johns' pubs are much diminished in number. One lost pub is the Beehive. An early twentieth-century licensee was a Mr Hopping, who also taught swimming at the Baths. The house was owned by Nicholsons of Maidenhead and later Courage, but was acquired by Morlands in 1992. Shortly afterwards it was sold off as private dwellings.

Above: The County Arms in Watlington Street was initially associated with the County Brewery, which flourished during the 1870s. In 1936 it was rebuilt by Morlands in the Brewer's Tudor style which was popular during this era. It is currently boarded up following sale by Greene King and refusal of planning permission for a housing development on the site.

Left: The Fishermans Cottage, Kennet Side, is a Grade II Listed Gothic folly, believed to date from around 1790. An American serviceman is said to have walked out of the pub during the Second World War and straight into the river. A Courage pub till the 1970s, it was then operated as a genuine free house for several years by 'Dr' Paul Hexter. After he sold it to Fullers it was extended at a reported cost of £150,000 and given a canal theme.

Right: Like other Brakspears pubs in Reading, the Dove at 119 Orts Road was originally a Greys Brewery pub. In this photograph, predating the takeover by a year or two, the signage shows the names Holmes and Steward, who were proprietors of the Greys Brewery prior to its acquisition by Brakspears in 1896. The landlord at this time was George Munday (depicted here).

Below: In more recent years, the Dove has suffered from numerous changes of management, only achieving brief stability during the 1990s when run by George and Rose Scott, formerly of the Retreat. An attempt to rebadge it as a gay pub in the new century evidently failed, and in 2006 the bulldozers moved in.

Left: Little seems to have been recorded of the Golden Lion, 54 Watlington Street, but to this day the Simonds hop leaf betrays its status as a former pub. At the end of the nineteenth century, John Jason Spyer was a grocer and the licensee.

Below: There is little at 39 St John's Road to suggest it was once the Lifeboat. On the north-west corner of the junction with St John's Hill, this modest beerhouse had Edwin Butcher, William George Saint and James Pike among its licensees in the late Victorian period.

Opposite: The Military Arms, Queens Road was kept by Mrs Clara Tyrrell in 1879, Edwin Deering in 1900 and Frederick Henry Beavis in 1914. It possibly derived its name from the Cannon Brewery that flourished on the site in the mid-nineteenth century. By 1971, it had become a grocers and it remains as a corner shop to this day, handy for patrons of the nearby Retreat.

Many characters have peopled the Retreat, including Moriarty, Military George and Barry the mouth-organ player. Here Raymond Quelch, who has shared many reminiscences with the author, is seen enjoying a pint.

Opposite above: One of the Reading pubs included in CAMRA's first *Good Beer Guide* in 1974 with many subsequent re-entries, the Retreat at 8 Street John's Street continues to merit the description 'a delightful back-street pub'. It became a pub in the later nineteenth century. Early landlords included Thomas Law and George Uzzle, and for many years it was owned by Wethered's.

Opposite below: The Retreat subsequently passed into the hands of Enterprise Inns, before being sold on to Admiral Taverns in 2006. Initially under Graham Mutton, and subsequently Peter Brookes, Bernie Whiten and Jane Marsden, it acquired a deserved reputation as a free house selling a good range of micro-brewed beers, as well as cider and foreign beer.

Above and below: The inn sign of the True Patriot displayed Churchill giving his 'V for Victory' sign. In 1972 a couple that regularly used the pub came in before midday. and found the landlady doing her ironing on the bar-counter. 'Sorry, I didn't expect any customers this soon' she exclaimed. It is seen here in splendid isolation as Newtown was dismantled about it, but it too met its end. The name remains, however, commemorated in Patriot Place on Orts Road.

The Cambridge Arms, Southampton Street, is listed as the Cambridge Inn in 1879, with Thomas Barton as landlord. A Fergusons house, it passed with their estate into Morlands' hands and was rebuilt in Brewer's Tudor style. For many years during and after the Second World War, it was run by a Mrs White. During the

period of rationing the pub was the scene of illicit meat sales. When a raid by Ministry of Food officials was threatened, the meat was hidden between layers of coal in the coal hole.

From the mid-1960s until 1989 it was run by Cecil and Lorna Bartlett, shown here at Christmas-tide. Lorna and Bart came from Maidenhead, making a wise investment of a win on the pools. In 1980 it became the author's local.

Like most pubs the Cambridge had its share of characters. Seen here are Jack Turner, with the tie, and his pal, George. Jack liked to bring in exotic species of snuff and share them with the regulars.

Joe the Bargee and Tony McKay indulging in the art of pipe-smoking.

Above and below: Bart and Lorna were followed for five years by a Scottish couple, Peter and Carol Shove. During this period, the Cambridge built up a fearsome reputation as a sporting pub. Its quiz team was twice overall winner of the coveted Morland Original Bitter League with cups, shields and certificates boldly displayed, and at one time there were as many as four bar billiards teams playing from the pub.

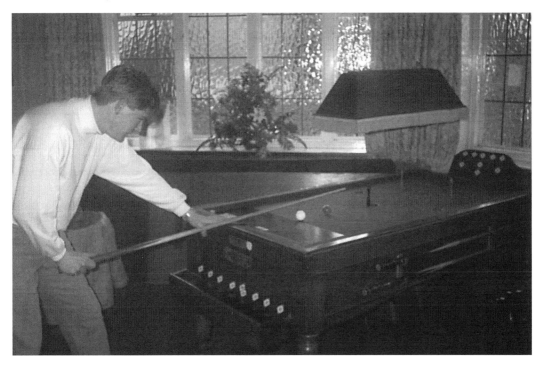

Unfortunately a succession of brief tenancies followed with the result that the pub was sold for conversion to private residences in 1998. This was carried out without planning permission, which was obtained retrogressively. The developer renamed the site Tudor Lodge, but in the process painted over the tiling and the Brewer's Tudor woodwork.

Opposite above: The Kennet Arms, Pell Street, has recently reverted to its old name having been called the Claddagh Ring from 1995. The pub was said to have had the coolest beer in Reading because of the proximity of its cellar to the river. In 1899, alterations and additions were undertaken to designs of James Hugh Goodman. In recent years it has been a favourite with the Irish community.

The Four Horseshoes, Basingstoke Road, was known as Long Barn, Whitley, early in the nineteenth century. Licensees have included Thomas Humphris, William Fabry, Charles Ransome and Mrs Ellen Ransome.

Subsequently rebuilt, in latter years the Four Horseshoes encountered trouble with the wild men of Whitley and is now an oriental restaurant.

● Protestors keep up the battle to save The Greyhound as council sends back plans for changes

Anti-demolition protestors claim pub's future isn't wrapped up

By Becki Dixon

ANGRY protesters who wrapped the Greyhound Pub in a red ribbon this week say they did it to demonstrate their disillusionment with Reading Borough Council.

The Silver Street pub is marked for demolition along with the British School in Southampton Street. Developer Beazer Homes hopes to build flats and a community centre on the site in partnership with the council.

Katesgrove Residents Influencing New Development (KIND) has been campaigning to block the development and presented a 400-signature petition to the council in July.

A spokesman said: "We're worried they will make a gift of Reading's history to the developers, Beazer Homes against the wishes of Katesgrove people.

"We're losing our history in Reading very rapidly and having it replaced by artificial heritage and token conservation."

Protestor Jackie Sturge, who lives in Newark Street, added: "There are a lot of us who feel very strongly about this. The flats will be four or five storeys high and there are a lot of residents who will be overlooked.

This week a council spokesman said planners have sent back Beazer's initial application asking for minor alterations.

She added: "After the initial consultation on the original plans there were some little amendments to be made, though they are nothing drastic. When the application comes back we will consult on the plans again. This is normal procedure."

Gifted: Members of Katesgrove Residents Influencing New Development make their mark on The Greyhound.

Despite vigorous protests, depicted here, the Greyhound, Mount Pleasant (originally Silver Street) was demolished in 2000 for a new housing development. In spite of its undoubted antiquity, listing was refused on grounds that it had been too much altered. It was run by the Scearce family, who also owned the adjoining blacksmith's forge for 125 years. In more recent years the most memorable landlord was Bill Mowbray, who sadly died from leukemia in 1990 after fourteen years at the helm.

The Hook & Tackle, Katesgrove Lane (originally Orchard Street), was called the Tanners Arms until 1984, with reference to the nearby Filberts Tannery.

Its proximity to the Kennet no doubt suggested the new name, which was adopted when it was acquired from Courage as a free house by Stephen Ellyatt, who was also landlord of the London Tavern. It was extended then at a cost of £40,000 and has since been further extended.

The Hop Leaf is currently one of the few pubs where bar billiards is preferred to pool. There are two teams, one of which was not very successfully captained by the author for several years.

Opposite above: The Hop Leaf, 163-65 Southampton Street, is a Grade II Listed building. George Benwell was beer retailer at this address in 1879. In 1907 the architectural firm of Millar & Cox was responsible for its 'rebuilding'. Darts has been played at the Hop Leaf since time immemorial.

Opposite below: Originally a Simonds pub, it was reopened in 1995 as a tied house of the Hopback Brewery, initially with a small brew plant operated by Eddie Robinson, who claimed to be the only brewer in the country of Maori descent. Mrs Nola Robinson was formerly a stalwart of the crib team.

Portrayed here by Timms, the Little Crown at 13 Southampton Street was prominent as a loading point and house of call for wagons, as featured in the picture. When the Beating of the Bounds party called there in 1816 they 'regaled

11 boys (who accompanied them) with bread and cheese and beer, at the Little Crown, and gave them a shilling each,' while the adults in the party refreshed themselves at the Crown. Before its demise in 1969 it hosted meetings of the local Model Racing Car Club.

In the eighteenth century it was the custom for the condemned man with his executioner to call at the Oxford Arms in Silver Street for his last drink on the way to Gallows Tree Common in Earley. According to William Darter it was 'kept by a man of the name of Fletcher' at the time the last recorded 'Hangman's Drink' took place in 1793. James Fletcher was still licensee in 1823.

Right: George Rose, landlord of the Oxford Arms for fifty years from 1909, recalled that, 'The rabbit poachers used to call into my pub – they used to bring three or four dozen rabbits about five times a week, about 7.30 in the morning and put them under the bar seat and sell them for about 4*d* and 6*d* each.' Some of these shady characters took a fox round on a lead.

Below: George Rose was well known in local boxing circles and a long term member of the Pilgrim Flying Club. He died, aged seventy-four, the year after the pub was demolished in 1959. In its heyday, pub outings from the Oxford Arms were evidently very popular.

Above: A Listed building with an attractive curved frontage, the Red Cow stands on the northern corner of Southampton Street and Crown Street. In the nineteenth and early twentieth centuries, licensees included Walter Dolman, John Easby, Henry Robert Hoskins, William Scearce, Richard Graham and Edward John Davenport.

Left: In the post-war era 'Jack the Hat' was landlord for many years. A veteran of the Burma campaign, he was rarely, if ever, seen without his eponymous hat and was still wearing his demob suit.

The Red Lion at 34 Southampton Street was formerly a Wethereds house and sometimes referred to as the Old Red Lion. Landlords from 1823 onwards included John Harbor, Richard Hall, Edwin Charles Medhurst, George Whatley and James Athersuch. Twenty years ago the pub was given a £130,000 refurbishment, completed in 1988.

The Red Rose has long ceased to be a pub, but the name is partly preserved in what is now Rose Cottage at 98-100 Southampton Street. This is a Grade II Listed building. James Neate and William Jack were beer retailers at the pub in the late nineteenth century and in the 1930s it was kept by two elderly sisters who demanded a penny in the swear box for bad language; if you did not pay up, you were barred!

Above: The Reindeer,
9 Southampton Street, was
run by William Samuel
Monger in 1887 and later
by a lady remembered as
'Sid Ballard's granny'. In her
day the pub used to open
at 6 a.m. so that workers
at nearby Simonds Brewery
could have a pint before work.
It closed in January 1969 and
was demolished to make way
for the IDR.

Left: In West Reading, the
former Cyprus Arms at
1 Derby Street is still trading
as the Elephant Off-Licence.
Also nearby was the Derby
Arms, a rare local outlet for
the Goring Brewery.

Above and below: The Foresters Arms in Brunswick Street was formerly a Justins-Brinn pub proclaiming the virtues of their 'Ales' and 'Celebrated Stout' and later owned successively by Dymore Brown and Morlands. With its fine tiled and Brewer's Tudor frontage and its unusual inn sign, it continues to trade as a free house and is also a rare example of a corridor pub.

Above: A spacious former Wethereds pub, the Pond House, 738 Oxford Road, was named after a pond that then existed on the opposite side of the Oxford Road.

Left: Also a Wethereds pub in times past, the Queen Elizabeth in George Street has had a chequered history of late with complaints of rowdy behaviour leading to loss of its licence. In 1953, the landlord commissioned local artist Jack West to paint a picture of the new Queen for display during the Coronation celebrations, but if this ever found its way onto the inn sign it was later replaced by the rather forbidding portrait of Good Queen Bess, as seen here.

The Rose & Thistle, Argyle Road is a Listed building. William Parsons was landlord in 1887 followed by Mrs Esther Mary Cole in 1914. Formerly a Courage pub, it was taken over first by Magic Pubs and then Greene King.

Here a more recent manageress of the Rose & Thistle, Hannah Sheahan, is shown washing cars in a charity stunt.

HORNCASTLE
BATH RD
READING

The Caversham Bridge Hotel began life as the White Hart and was for a while was owned by Ann Freebody of the boat-building family. In 1878, it was acquired by Antonio Giovanni Bona who agreed to rebuild it in order to permit the old Caversham Bridge to be replaced. The rebuilding finally took place in 1901 to the design of G.W. Webb, but the bridge itself was not replaced until 1924. It closed in 1986 to make way for a Holiday Inn.

Opposite above: The Horncastle on Bath Road, Calcot, is on the very edge of Reading's new boundaries, drawn in 1911 when Tilehurst and Caversham were brought into the borough. In the eighteenth century it was associated with the story of the 'Berkshire Lady', Miss Kendrick, who married her husband after ambushing him disguised as a man outside the old inn. It was later rebuilt in the roadhouse style.

Opposite below: Lord Byng described 'the well-placed public house, the Roe Buck, where all the fishing parties of the neighbourhood dine'. Rebuilt in the nineteenth century, the Roebuck was used as a meet for the Berkshire Hunt and the future King Edward VII is said to have been among the huntsmen. It is claimed to be haunted by an unnamed admiral who was burnt to death looking for his faithful hound which had wisely escaped out of the window of the blazing pub. During the early part of the First World War, the field opposite was used as a training ground for horses before they went into battle.

The Crown, Caversham Bridge, was rebuilt when the new bridge was built in 1926. Prior to that, its proprietors included George Barefoot, Albert Edward Hulbert and various members of the Andress family.

Opposite above: The great claim to fame of the Fox & Hounds at 51 Gosbrook Road is that in 1960 it was run by Mike Robbins and wife, Bett, who was a cousin of the young Paul McCartney. The future Sir Paul visited the pub with John Lennon, and as payment for working behind the bar the two proto-Beatles were allowed to perform in the pub for two nights!

Opposite below: There has been an inn on the site of the Griffin in Church Road, Caversham, since the early seventeenth century, the sign of the griffin being part of the coat of arms of Lord Craven, then Lord of the Manor. In 1723, Jonathan Blagrave, a wealthy farmer, bragged too loudly of his profitable visit to market and was bludgeoned to death some 300 yards from the inn on his way home at 3 a.m. The old inn shown here was demolished and rebuilt in 1911.

The Prince of Wales in Prospect Street, formerly Little End, Caversham, was another pub that passed to Brakspears with the Greys Brewery estate in 1896. The pub was the terminus of an early omnibus service to the Elephant Inn, Market Place via Caversham Bridge and Greyfriars Road.

4

SOME NEW PUBS

The massacre of public houses that has been recorded in these pages has been partly compensated by many new pubs created in recent memory, mostly converted from existing retail premises and heritage sites. The Bel and the Dragon at Blakes Lock was a conversion of parts of an old pumping station that had previously housed a folk museum into a high-class pub/restaurant. The name unfortunately perhaps duplicates that of the once unique ancient inn in Cookham village.

Left: The Great Expectations, 33 London Street, began life as the Mechanics' Institution around 1840. It was designed by William Brown (1809-65), who also designed Reading's first cemetery. It became a pub in 1998, having served in the meantime as a Primitive Methodist Chapel, a theatre and a small business centre. Dickens was president of the institution and gave several of his readings here – hence the new name.

Below: The Happy Prospect on the Southcote estate is typical of a number of new pubs which have been plagued by poor management and violent customers, mostly leading to their demise.

Right and below: The former Congregational Chapel, Castle Street, built in the late 1830s, closed for worship in 1956 and served as a furniture store and Mexican restaurant-cum-night club before becoming a pub at the turn of the century. Originally the Litten Tree, it is now known as Dogma.

The Mansion House in Prospect Park, Liebenrood Road, was originally a real mansion known as Prospect Hill House and associated with the eighteenth-century femme fatale, Frances Kendrick, 'the Berkshire Lady'. The building passed into the ownership of the council in 1901 and after falling into disrepair from the 1950s was restored by Whitbread as a Brewer's Fayre pub/restaurant.

Opposite above: The Monk's Retreat, 163 Friar Street, opened as J.D. Wetherspoon's first Reading outlet in 1994, in what had been a TV shop. It is not far from the site of Reading Abbey and features the life-size monk seen here swinging from the ceiling on a bellrope. Three other Wetherspoons now grace the town, including the Baron Cadogan in Caversham.

Getting into a happy habit at The Monks' Retreat

Managers Eugene Docherty and Shirley Murphy enjoy a drink with one of their regulars at The Monks' Retreat in Reading.

The pub, on the site of a former electrical store in the centre of town, features two sculptures. The second depicts a monk disappearing up a bell rope.

The Monks' Retreat takes its name from the monks who lived in the nearby Abbey, which at one time was the largest and wealthiest Benedictine monastery in the country.

Wetherspoon's spent £700,000 converting the site into a two bar pub, with one bar designated as a non-smoking area.

Shirley said: "We've only been open for a short time, but already the pub is proving a great success.

"The two sculptures are a great attraction and have created a lot of interest from our customers."

Right: Sweeney & Todd, 10 Castle Street, is an almost unique Reading institution that trebles as a delicatessen, restaurant and bar and is famous for its infinite range of succulent pies. Formerly a butcher's shop, it acquired its present status in the 1970s under Reading butcher, Alan Hayward. The barber shop next door was a later arrival on the scene, formerly a Post Office.

Yates's Wine Lodge in Friar Street took over the premises of the town's main Post Office, which was built on the site of the former Queen's Hotel. Legend has it that on one occasion a disaffected customer chucked a block of stone through the window and the bouncers threw themselves to the floor. It is a far cry from the old Queen's, Tory HQ during elections where proprietor, Mary Elisabeth George 'held autocratic sway' and whose distinguished guests included the Maharajah of Gooch Behar with his six wives!

Opposite: The Zerodegrees group of micro-brewpub/restaurants opened their Reading outlet in early 2007, brewing and retailing continental style beers which immediately notched up an award at the Reading Beer Festival. The photo shows the site under construction.

With so many pubs closing it is good to record one that has reopened – and as a real pub. The Magpie & Parrot in Shinfield just outside Reading closed about sixty years ago to become a farmhouse but never lost its licence. Reopened by Carole Headland as a sideline to her nurseries business, it has become a regular *Good Beer Guide* entry and winner of CAMRA awards.

5

THE BREWERIES

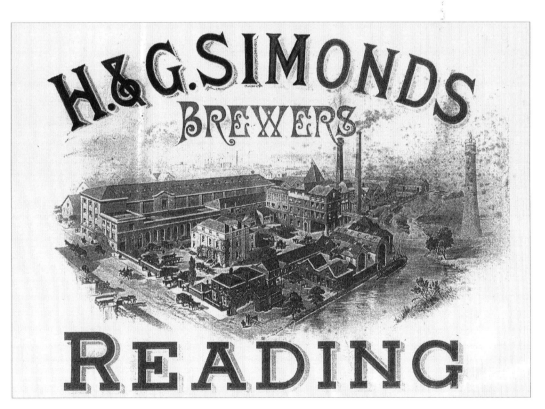

Reading was for long an important centre of brewing although the last major brewery, Scottish Courage, produces only processed beers. It is the successor to the great Simonds Brewery, founded in 1785 and pictured here in its mid-Victorian heyday. This image has been used as the basis for a commemorative board about the brewery erected within the Oracle development by Reading Civic Society and members of the Simonds family.

Above and opposite: Simonds was known for its trademark of a hop leaf, shown here at the Magpie & Parrot, Shinfield. It was said to have been designed for Simonds by his friend, Sir John Soane, who also designed the Bridge Street Brewery. The hop leaf motif was also used to promote its well known keg brand, Tavern.

Ask for

TAVERN
INDIA PALE ALE

The old brewery is shown here shortly before its demolition. Brewing ceased at the Bridge Street site in 1979. Its successor, known as the Berkshire Brewery, was closed in 2010 by new owners, Heineken.

Opposite above and below: Dymore Brown began brewing in Castle Street, but moved to its new Royal Albert Brewery in Queens Road in 1864. The company was eventually acquired by Morlands who used the brewery for bottling until 1961. It was later used as a garage, but following a severe fire in 1990 the buildings were demolished.

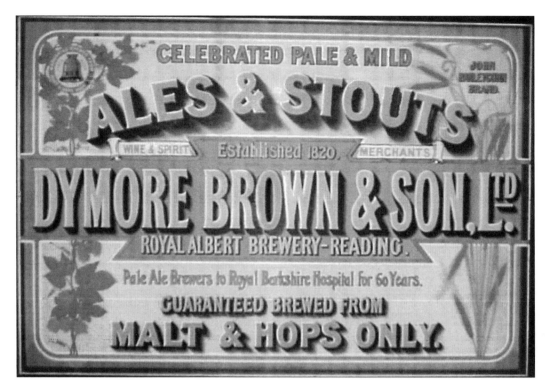

The firm specialised in providing beers to great houses, where it was often drunk 'below stairs', and public institutions such as the Royal Berkshire Hospital. A far cry from the attitude to beer of today's medics! At its height its output was 14,000 barrels per annum.

Opposite: One of the smaller Reading brewers, S.H. Higgs, was located at the Lion Brewery and Tap in Castle Street.

HIGGS' LION BREWERY

Above and opposite: Originally operated by James Moore, the Lion Brewery was taken over by Samuel Higgs in 1877 but was bought out by Wethereds of Marlow with eight houses in 1953. Latterly it had some of the best advertising – their adverts can be found in Reading Football Club programmes too – and the prices look good.

Through the takeover of Dymore Brown, Fergusons and Hewitts Morlands of Abingdon became the largest supplier of beer in Reading after Simonds. Itself the victim of a takeover by Greene King in 1999, its familiar artist ceramic plaques can still be seen on many pubs in and around the town.

"Can you beat this for good BEER— Well, it's HIGGS"

"You should get some for Christmas"

HIGGS' DRAUGHT BEER,
3½d. PINT.

On Sale in all their houses.

PHONE
READING
3681

= IN BOTTLE =

	4 Quarts	Doz. qts.	Doz. ½-pts.
DINNER ALE	2/10	5/-	—
PALE ALE	3/4	5/6	—
INDIAN P. ALE	4/4	7/-	4/-
LIGHT LUNCHEON	3/-	5/3	—
DOUBLE STOUT	4/4	7/-	4/-
MILK STOUT ...	5/-	8/-	4/6
GUINNESS & BASS	—	9/-	5/-
CIDER	2/3	6/-	3/6
GINGER BEER ...	2/3	—	2/6

= IN CASK =

B.B.	pin 8/3 ... firkin	16/6
F.P.A.	9/3 ...	18/6
I.P.A.	14/3	28/6
A.K.	11/6	23/-

HIGGS

Deliveries to all parts daily.

THE LION BREWERY, READING.

Howard Bull Advertising.

MORLAND & CO., LIMITED

MAXIMUM PUBLIC BAR PRICES

DRAUGHT			Pint	Half pint
MILD	:	:	1/7	9½d.
BITTER	:	:	1/9	10½d.
BEST BITTER	:		2/1	1/0½
BASS	:	:	2/2	1/1

BOTTLED			Large	Small	Nip
LIGHT ALE	:		2/-	1/1	-
BROWN ALE	:		2/-	1/1	-
STOUT	:	:	2/-	1/1	-
BEAGLE	:	:	-	1/4	-
VIKING	:	:	-	1/5½	-
MONARCH	:		-	-	1/8½
WHITBREAD	:		-	1/4½	-
FOREST BROWN			-	1/4½	-
MACKESON	:		-	1/8	-
GUINNESS	:		3/3	1/8	1/4
BASS	:	:	-	1/8½	1/4
WORTHINGTON			-	1/8½	1/4
BASS BARLEY WINE			-	-	2/-

THE BREWERY, ABINGDON

A Morlands price list from the 1960s, photographed at the North Star, Steventon.

Opposite: Another out of town brewer with pubs in Reading was Nicholson's of Maidenhead. It was acquired by Courage in 1959, the year before they also bought out Simonds.

BIBLIOGRAPHY

The following books are among those consulted by the author in his research for this book:

Byng, John (1996) *Rides Round Britain* (Folio Society)

Defoe, Defoe (1724) *Tour through the Whole Island of Britain* (1971 edition) (Penguin English Library)

Darter, William (1889) *Memoirs of an Octogenarian* (1985 edition, Daphne Phillips Ed.) (Countryside Books)

Dils, Joan (Ed.) *Reading Turnpikes* (Manuscript)

Ditchfield, P.H. (1887) *Reading Seventy Years Ago* (Reading)

Dix, Frank (1985) *Royal River Highway* (David & Charles)

Dormer, Ernest (1937) *The Story of Royal Berkshire Hospital, 1837-1937* (Poynder Press)

Gold, Sidney (1999) *Biographical Dictionary of Architects at Reading* (Privately Published)

Guilding, Reverend J.M. (Ed.) (1895) *Diary of the Corporation, 4 vols.* (James Parker)

Hadland, Tony (1992) *Thames Valley Papists* (Privately Published)

Long, Roger (1996) *Ancient Berkshire Inns and their Stories* (TWM Publishing)

Mitford, Mary Russell (1835) *Belford Regis* (1945 edition) (T. Werner Laurie)

Padley, Fred (1983) *Village in a Town* (Reading WEA)

Pudney, John (1971) *Draught of Contentment* (New English Library)

Reading Libraries (1974) *Inns of Reading* (Reading Libraries)

Smart, James (Ed.) (2007) *London Street Described* (London Street Research Group)

Sowan, Adam (2005) *Abattoirs Road to Zinzan Street* (Two Rivers Press)

Thirkell, John (1973) *400 Glorious Pubs* (Imprint)

Wykes, Alan (1970) *Reading, A Biography* (MacMillan)

Other titles published by The History Press

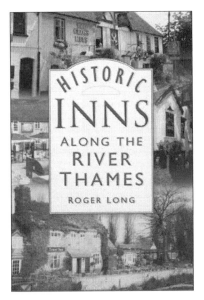

Historic Inns along the River Thames
ROGER LONG

Around ninety inns are featured here, with potted histories, illustrations and directions on how to find them. The book begins at the source and wends its way along the course of the river, eventually working its way to the sea. This is a book of romantic accounts concerning authors, poets and artists, a cople of horrific murders and comical stories. Colourful anecdotes about charismatic landlords, tales of highwaymen and love stories concerning eloping landlords' daughters also feature, along with historical accouns of royal patronages.

978 0 7509 4364 5

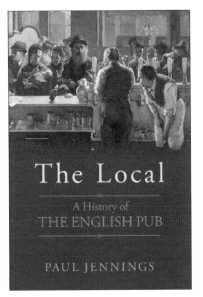

The Local: A History of the English Pub
PAUL JENNINGS

Paul Jennings traces the history of the British pub, and looks at how it evolved from the eighteenth-century coaching inns and humble alehouses, back-street beerhouses and 'fine, flaring' gin palaces to the drinking establishments of the twenty-first century. Covering all aspects of pub life, this fascinating history looks at pubs in cities and rural areas, seaports and industrial towns. From music and games to opening times, this is a must-read for every self-respecting pub-goer, from landlady to lager-lout.

978 0 7524 3994 5

Reading Football Club 1871-1997

COMPILED BY DAVID DOWNS

From its foundation as a team for local amateur enthusiasts, to its emergence as a major English club, this collection of over 200 photographs traces the history of Reading Football Club. But the book illustrates more than just the players and matches; it features the backroom staff, the supporters, all kinds of memorabilia, programmes and some unusual and amusing incidents. This is a book that will fascinate all supporters, past and present, young and old.

978 0 7524 1061 6

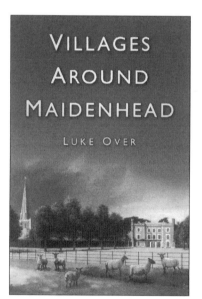

Villages Around Maidehead

LUKE OVER

Maidenhead came into being no earlier than the thirteenth century, yet the many of the surrounding villages and manors were well-established by the Domesday Survey of 1086. Here, information is brought together from the *Domesday Book*, parish records, ancient civic rolls, analysis of place names and fieldwork to describe the development of these settlements, and the people that made them. Luke Over is an historian and archaeologist with fifty years working knowledge in the Maidenhead area. His exceptional understanding of the area, along with his vibrant enthusiasm makes this a fascinating read for all those interested in the development of modern Maidenhead.

978 0 7524 5289 0

Visit our website and discover thousands of other History Press books.

www.thehistorypress.co.uk

The History Press